MEDITERRANEAN DIET FOR BEGINNERS:

The Ultimate Mediterranean Cookbook with Amazing Recipes to Help Improve Your Health and Discover True Mediterranean Cuisine

©Copyright 2018 by Andrea Gianakouli All rights reserved.

The follow eBook is reproduced below with the goal of providing information that is as accurate and reliable as possible. Regardless, purchasing this eBook can be seen as consent to the fact that both the publisher and the author of this book are in no way experts on the topics discussed within and that any recommendations or suggestions that are made herein are for entertainment purposes only. Professionals should be consulted as needed prior to undertaking any of the action endorsed herein.

This declaration is deemed fair and valid by both the American Bar Association and the Committee of Publishers Association and is legally binding throughout the United States.

Furthermore, the transmission, duplication or reproduction of any of the following work including specific information will be considered an illegal act irrespective of if it is done electronically or in print. This extends to creating a secondary or tertiary copy of the work or a recorded copy and is only allowed with express written consent from the Publisher. All additional right reserved.

The information in the following pages is broadly considered to be a truthful and accurate account of facts, and as such any inattention, use or misuse of the information in question by the reader will render any resulting actions solely under their purview. There are no scenarios in which the publisher or the original author of this work can be in any fashion deemed liable for any hardship or damages that may befall them after undertaking information described herein.

Additionally, the information in the following pages is intended only for informational purposes and should thus be thought of as universal. As befitting its nature, it is presented without assurance regarding its prolonged validity or interim quality. Trademarks that are mentioned are done without written consent and can in no way be considered an endorsement from the trademark holder.

Disclaimer

All content in this book including images, text, and all other formats are provided for informational purposes only. It is not intended, in any way, to be a substitute for the professional medical diagnosis, treatment, or advice. You should always seek medical advice from a healthcare professional with any question you may have regarding a medical condition.

Table of Contents

Introduction.......6

Chapter 1 What is The Mediterranean Diet? 8

Chapter 2 History of the Mediterranean Diet.......17

Chapter 3 Mediterranean Diet: Colors, Taste & Health.......29

Chapter 4 Popular Foods Of The Mediterranean Diet.......40

Chapter 5 Benefits Of The Mediterranean Diet.......65

Chapter 6 Meal Plans For A Week.......77

Conclusion.......127

Introduction

Congratulations on downloading this book and thank you for doing so.

The following chapters will discuss the Mediterranean diet in great detail. This book will show you how to follow the Mediterranean lifestyle for ultimate health and wellbeing.

The Mediterranean diet has been touted as the healthiest lifestyle in the world. This is because it offers clean eating with a focus on natural products. Eating natural, healthy foods everyday will not just boost your health but will enable your body to fight infections, keep chronic conditions at bay, and increase longevity.

You will learn which foods you need to eat if you want to lose weight, which foods are excellent for keeping infections at bay and how to combat inflammation. Eating naturally comes easy, and the Mediterranean diet makes it even easier with its delicious and tasty meals.

There are plenty of books on this subject on the market, thanks again for choosing this one! Every effort was made to ensure it is full of as much useful information as possible, please enjoy!

Chapter1: What is the Mediterranean Diet?

The Mediterranean diet is a diet that is based on the traditional foods that communities in countries along the Mediterranean used to eat in the 1930s to 1960s. These countries include Spain, Italy, and Greece.

According to researchers, communities living along the Mediterranean have exceptionally low risk regarding lifestyle diseases compared to Americans. Numerous studies have been conducted and they all show that the Mediterranean diet is beneficial to our health and wellbeing. Observing this diet regularly will help prevent conditions such as strokes, heart attacks, type II diabetes, as well as premature death.

The World's Healthiest Diet

There are those that have claimed that the Mediterranean diet is one of the healthiest diets in the world. This is mainly because of the kinds of foods involved. This diet includes whole grains, vegetables, fruits, olive oil, legumes, and proteins like seafood and fish. Red meat is rarely consumed and perhaps only once a week or even a fortnight.

This diet focuses on foods and normal recipes of the Mediterranean style of cooking. While the Mediterranean diet is not your typical, run-of-the-mill diet, it is actually a lifestyle. You can think of it as a different way of eating and living. Following this lifestyle, you are able to make well-balanced food choices that boost your health and taste great while promoting weight loss and development of lean muscle.

Major Components of the Mediterranean Diet

If you wish to follow the Mediterranean diet lifestyle, then you need to understand its key components. These include the following;

- Eating mostly plant-based foods such as green leafy vegetables, fruits, and whole grains.
- Replacing butter and margarine with healthy oils like olive oil.
- Making use of spices and herbs for flavoring rather than salt.
- Eating moderate portions of poultry and eggs once a week or every two days.
- Limiting your intake of red meats to either weekends or a couple of times per month. You can also limit red meat consumption to three-ounce portions.
- Eating fish or fish products at least two times weekly.
- Having moderate sizes of yogurt and cheese daily, every other day or weekly.
- Drinking a lot of water each day.
- Drink some red wine but in moderation.

Even as you follow this healthy diet, you should avoid the unhealthy foods and ingredients indicated below. To be on the safe side, make sure that you read the labels carefully to identify and avoid these unhealthy foods.

- ***Refined grains***: These include pasta made from refined grains and white bread.
- ***Refined oils***: These include soybean oil, cottonseed oil, and canola oil.
- ***Added sugars:*** For instance, avoid ice cream, candies, soda, and table sugar.
- ***Trans fats:*** Make sure you find substitutes for butter and margarine.
- ***Processed meats:*** They include ham, sausages, hot dogs, and so on.
- ***Highly processed foods:*** Foods you buy at the grocery store as well as any items labeled **"diet"** or **"low fat"** and those that are processed at a factory.

Research into Mediterranean Diet

There is a lot of research that has been carried out on this diet. Most of the research examined the benefits and health implications. According to findings, following the Mediterranean diet lifestyle has been found to be very beneficial to human health. Researchers found that this diet helps to reduce levels of inflammation in the body. Inflammation is a risk factor for conditions such as stroke, heart attack, and Alzheimer's.

Other notable attributes of this lifestyle include better blood sugar regulation, improved weight loss, and reduced cancer risk, lower chances of depression and many others. All these claims have been closely examined and proven to be correct.

Numerous Diet Plans Out There

There are numerous diets plans out there. Many of these are restrictive. They put a limit on what you can eat or drink and what you cannot. The problem with these diets is not just the restrictions but also the temporary nature of outcomes. If you wish to lose weight, a diet plan can help you lose weight which you regain once you are done with it.

The good news is that the Mediterranean diet is not simply a diet but a lifestyle. If you choose this diet as a lifestyle, then you can expect to lose weight and keep it off. You will also enjoy all the other benefits of this lifestyle. The Mediterranean diet will not require that you drop everything that you love and appreciate about food. Rather, you are permitted to make simple changes to your diet over time to make it a lifestyle and not a challenge.

Fortunately, the Mediterranean diet is different. It is a lifestyle and diet that mimics the life and eating habits of people living in places like Southern Italy and Greece in the 1940s, 1950s, and 1960s.

Rather than go on a diet for a fixed period of time, you will mostly endeavor to eat meals or dishes that are high in the foods already discussed above. These include unrefined cereals, moderate consumption of dairy products, low consumption of red meat and other non-fish meat products.

Evidence-Based Benefits

There is evidence available that this diet actually lowers your risk of heart and cardiovascular disease and even death. It is believed that olive oil is the major ingredient that promotes health in this diet.

This diet has become so significant that the United Nations, through its cultural branch, UNESCO, has identified this diet as an inherent part of the culture of countries across the Mediterranean including Croatia, Cyprus, Greece, Portugal, Morocco, and Spain.

The United Nations chose this diet because it involves a lot of symbols, knowledge, traditions, rituals, and skills concerning food processing, cooking, fishing, animal husbandry, crops harvesting and even the sharing and consumption of food.

About the Mediterranean Diet

This diet offers you a cuisine that is rich in flavors, colors, aromas, taste, and memories. The diet also supports the spirit and taste of all those who are in harmony with nature.

Not many people know how to correctly follow this diet and the associated lifestyle. While many talks about the Mediterranean diet, only a few follows it properly. This tends to generate a lot of confusion. Some think it constitutes a pizza with some meat or seafood, others think it is all about noodles and meat.

However, the Mediterranean diet is simple yet very healthy. A good diet aims to combine and balance food such that it satisfies the quantitative and qualitative needs of a person. In essence, a good diet is more of a lifestyle thana way of eating. It helps to preserve good health by making use of nutrients that enable the body to perform optimally all its vital functions.

This diet shows that it is possible to combine the goodness and taste of a meal ensuring it also provides health benefits. Consumers can be guaranteed of a dish that is delicious and tasty, yet still healthy and nutritious. Studies have consistently proven that Mediterranean cuisines make use of a wide variety of tasty food choices that include strong scents and inviting colors that are all in line with excellent health.

Chapter 2: History of the Mediterranean Diet

Historical Origins of the Mediterranean Diet

The Mediterranean basin covers more than 22 countries in Europe, Africa, and Asia. The diet of the communities living around this basin consists abundantly of plant foods like whole grains, legumes, seeds and nuts, olive oil, and fresh fruits and vegetables. There are only a few regional differences of this diet,and these differences are of little consequence to the diet because of numerous similarities. The origins of this diet reflect on the intricate interactions of civilizations and diverse populations over centuries.

Traditional Mediterranean Diet

The diet of the people living in the countries surrounding the Mediterranean Sea, such as Morocco, Spain, Greece, Italy and France were thought to be a poor man's diet. This traditional diet largely developed over thousands of years. The inhabitants of these lands labored to produce food and sustenance very poor terrain.

Some of the plants that grew here include grapevines, olive trees, and capers/ capers have an intense flavor. The olive tree is a symbolic plant that symbolizes all the plants growing in the region. It is also significant to the three largest religions of the Mediterranean. These are Christianity, Islam, and Judaism.

The local dishes of the Mediterranean were largely influenced by a rich history of different ethnic cultures from Italian to Spanish to Arabian. This region has for centuries been a center for culture and a crossroad for civilizations. As early as 3000 B.C., the region was occupied by Carthaginians, Romans, and Phoenicians among others.

Traditional Dishes over the Years

Traditional meals back then were heavily influenced by culture and foods available. Most of the dishes consisted of seafood, potatoes, eggplant, and tomatoes. The foods were flavored with spices originating mostly from North Africa. Families simply looked at their gardens to determine what to eat for dinner. The dishes then were very simple. They consisted mainly of local ingredients because importing food back then was very expensive. Sugar, for instance, was expensive to import, so they used honey and natural sweeteners instead.

While there was plenty of fish and seafood in their diets, residents of the Mediterranean coast were more of farmers than fishermen. Even then, iconic dishes such as pesto were common. They were made of garlic, raw tomatoes, olive oil and basil. Another iconic dish is fish couscous. It consists of a wide variety of vegetables, local seafoods, and legumes. Pantescan salad is a salad that was made with red onions, tomatoes, potatoes, and capers.

Caponata was a popular dish that consists of capers, eggplant, and olive oil. All these local dishes were common across the Mediterranean with small variations here and there. All these local foods are full of flavor, rich, and hearty. They are flavored with wild herbs, olive oil, and capers.

Public Acknowledgement of Mediterranean Diet

The Mediterranean diet was first publicly acknowledged by Ancel Keys, an American biologist, and his wife, Margaret Keys, a chemist in 1960s. However, it did not quite gain publicity or widespread recognition until the early 1990s. Studies from cities such as Madrid in Spain and Naples in Italy were the first sources of information on the usefulness and benefits of this diet.

Studies were conducted across the seven main countries of the Mediterranean and published in the 1970s. A report released in the 1980s closely followed the studies. Walter Willett of Harvard University's School of Public Health is credited as being the first person to produce a widely accepted version of the Mediterranean Diet. His publication was released in the mid-1990s.

High Amounts of Fat Consumed

Researchers participating in this study were amazed by the high amounts of fat the residents of Mediterranean countries consume. This is why most people at the time thought it was a paradox. The paradox is that these people tend to consume high amounts of fat but have some of the lowest rates of heart and cardiovascular diseases compared to people living in America.

Back then, people were amazed at this paradox mostly because of the high amounts of fat consumed but almost no signs of heart disease. In countries far from the Mediterranean such as England, residents consumed high levels of fats but were not as healthy. This is what was referred to as the French Paradox.

The French Paradox

The French Paradox is simply a catchphrase that was first used in the 1980s. This phrase refers to the apparent paradox based on observation. French citizens were found to have low levels of heart and cardiovascular conditions despite consuming a diet that is rich in saturated fats.

This was in great contrast to the general acceptance at the time that regular consumption of foods rich in saturated fats is a high-risk factor for coronary heart disease and other cardiovascular diseases. The paradox in this instance is that if the science linking saturated fats to coronary heart disease is true, then the French ought to have significantly high instances of heart diseases compared to countries where diets consist of low amounts of saturated fats.

Two possibilities are implied in the French Paradox. One possibility is that there exists a link between coronary heart disease and saturated fats, but the French lifestyle or diet mitigates against the risk. If this factor is identified, then it could explain the paradox. The other possibility is that no valid hypothesis links saturated fats to coronary heart disease.

The presumption with this paradox is that if the factor that mitigates the risk is identified, and then it can be applied to diets and lifestyles in other countries. This could help save lives so that people are healthier just like the French.

The French Diet

It has been observed over the years that the French diet lacks Trans fats is quite rich in short-chain saturated fatty acids. A researcher known as Frank Cooper noted in his book, "***Cholesterol and the French Paradox***," that the French Paradox is really because there are no Tran's fats and hydrogenated fats in the French diet.

There is a huge difference between the French and American diets. The American diet consists largely of huge amounts of hydrogenated vegetable oils while the French diet consists of natural saturated fats such as that found in cheese, nuts, and cream. These are easy for the human body to metabolize. The hydrogenated fats common in the American diet are difficult to metabolize and are associated with certain health risks.

Comparing the French Diet to the Mediterranean Diet

- People of the Mediterranean get almost 80% of their fats directly from vegetable and dairy sources such as cheese, whole milk, and whole milk yogurt. This shows the diet consists mostly of good fats. Americans, on the other hand, consume mostly unhealthy hydrogenated fats.
- Mediterranean people consume much higher quantities of fish compared to Americans. Fish contain healthy oils that contain omega 2 fatty acids.

- They eat smaller portions and divide their meals into courses. This allows food already consumed to be digested before more food is added.
- They also prefer products with full fat but without added sugar. They generally have a lower sugar intake. Americans consume large amounts of sugar directly and indirectly. Most no-fat and low-fat foods usually contain large amounts of sugar.
- The Mediterranean residents consume fewer snacks between meals. They also tend to avoid unhealthy options like carbonated drinks, snacks, deep fried foods, and most processed foods.
- They eat three meals per day but without snacking at all.
- They consume sufficient amounts of water, soups, and herbal tea.
- They prefer small quantities of high-quality food compared to Americans who sometimes prefer large amounts of low-quality foods.
- The Mediterranean people always seat down to eat their meals and savor each mouthful.

- They focus more on balance, freshness, variety, and pleasure.

Aspects of the Mediterranean Diet

1. Whole Diet – Scientists have noted that it is not a single nutrient that makes the Mediterranean diet so beneficial but rather a combination of nutrients that are inherent in unprocessed foods such as fruits, vegetables, nuts, and so on. In fact, the Mediterranean diet did not really focus on the amount of protein or fats consumed but the entire content of nutrients in a meal as sourced from natural foods. The focus was never on processed foods but only natural foods.

2. Greater Vegetable and Fruit - It has now become evident that a higher intake of vegetables and fruits in a diet will significantly reduce the risk of cardiovascular diseases.

3. Early Life Nutrition – Another reason why the Mediterranean diet is thought to be superior to the American diet is largely due to the dietary improvements within a child's early years of life.

Dietary improvements are extended to kids throughout the generations.

Some governments made a deliberate effort to introduce aggressive nutrition programs that provide excellent nutrition and quality foods to young children and pregnant women to have a healthy population. This great nutrition goes on to explain the low levels of heart disease and obesity across countries bordering the Mediterranean.

The Mediterranean Diet in Portugal

Researchers studying this diet compared it to the American diet and diets of developed countries. During the study, some researchers referred to the Mediterranean diet as the diet of the poor. The researchers also thought that Portugal had the purest form of the Mediterranean diet. The problem is that, back then in the 1960s and 1970s, the dictator of Portugal did not want his country associated with the diet of the poor.

The Portuguese preferred to refer to their diet as the "**Atlantic Diet**." This diet is really the

Mediterranean diet but with lots more seafood, fish, and green leafy vegetables.

Chapter 3: Mediterranean Diet: Colors, Taste, & Health

The Mediterranean diet has its origins in the Mediterranean basin. Some scientists consider this region to be the cradle of society. This is because the history of the ancient world actually took place here. More advanced civilizations such as the Egyptians existed across the Mediterranean along the banks of the Nile River.

According to the United Nation's cultural body UNESCO, the Mediterranean diet is defined as a lifestyle, a way of life, and a social practice. It involves knowledge and traditions ranging from fishing, cultures, conservation, harvesting, processing, fishing, preparation, and cooking food in a particular way.

Mediterranean Food Model

The Mediterranean diet is also known primarily as a food model. It enhances the safety and quality of food as well as links to the land. The meals offer a basic cuisine that is rich in taste, flavors, and nutrition. It takes total advantage of all the aspects of what is considered to be a healthy diet. This diet is ideally an ethical choice that maintains the customs and traditions of the inhabitants of the Mediterranean basin.

Consuming this diet on a regular basis is absolutely nourishing. It does have a profound effect on the health of an individual. The good nutrition involved helps to prevent metabolic diseases like hypertension, diabetes, and obesity. The Mediterranean diet does affect the health of families and communities because quality nutrition helps to maintain excellent health level and prevent diseases. Experts are of the opinion this diet is a useful resource that enables sustainable development which is superbly useful to the nations living around the Mediterranean and all over the world and also the cultural and economic effect of food.

Colors, Flavors, and Health at Center of the Mediterranean Diet

A lot of the health benefits associated with the Mediterranean diet can be attributed to Ancel Keys, an American research scientist from the University of Minnesota. She is the expert who was able to identify the correlation between this diet and cardiovascular diseases. Her research was as a result of intrigues because the relatively poor residents of the Mediterranean region were a lot healthier than their much wealthier counterparts in major cities like New York and London.

Keys pondered about this for a while and decided that it had something to do with the food and this is the reason why he led an expedition to learn more about the Mediterranean diet. Results for the study concluded that the diet actually presented a very low cholesterol rate in the blood. Because of this, people suffered less from the heart and coronary conditions. The main reason for this was the regular use of products such as pasta, olive oil, vegetables, bread, garlic, herbs, and red onions among numerous others. Also, most of the products used were of vegetable origin with very little use of red meat.

This was not the only study conducted by American scientists. It is safe to state that numerous other studies were conducted on the health benefits of the Mediterranean diet. There were points of convergence derived from these studies. One of these was the total recognition of the numerous beneficial qualities of this way of eating and living. Numerous studies as well clinical studies have repeatedly shown the many benefits and advantages of the Mediterranean diet. This is why it is viewed more as a lifestyle than a diet by many.

Of notable benefit is the diet's ability to reduce abdominal circumference, increase good cholesterol or HDL, reduce the presence of dangerous fats or triglycerides, reduces blood sugar levels, and also lowers blood pressure. It is important to note that the diet on its own will not be able to produce these amazing results. It is important to note that these benefits are not automatic, and people have to take deliberate steps to enjoy these benefits. Some risk factors have to be modified.

Some of the important factors that need to be modified include regular physical activity, quitting smoking, intake of sufficient but not excess calories and so on. It is also important to control any metabolic diseases such as obesity, diabetes, and hypertension. Leading a stress-free life or at least managing stress appropriately is definitely advisable. Eating a balanced diet and generally leading a disciplined lifestyle is absolutely recommended.

Middle Ages

Ancient Roman traditions greatly influenced the diet of the communities living along the Mediterranean coast. Some of the foods associated with Roman and Greek influence include wine, bread, and oil products. These were also seen as the symbols of the rural culture back then. This food options back then also included sheep cheese, seafood, fish, a variety of vegetables like lettuce, mallow, mushrooms, chicory, and leeks, and a little bit of red meat.

Not far from here, in the Germanic regions, pig fat was used for cooking and the little grain produced was not used for food but fermented to produce beer. These were introduced into the Mediterranean region but were not assimilated by the population. However, across the Mediterranean were the Arab lands of Morocco and others. The Arab and Muslim regions had developed their own food culture which was rather unique.

A lot of the foods within the Mediterranean diet are derived from the Islamic influence of the Mediterranean region. Muslims introduced agriculture to the region and derived a lot of their food from it. Some of the food crops they cultivated include eggplant, rice, citrus, sugar cane, spices, and spinach. Their cuisines consisted of other products from

Europe such as almonds, lemons, orange, rose water, and pomegranates.

It is clear, therefore, to observe how foods from European hinterland were unable to influence the Mediterranean diet but Muslim and North African food cultures did. Later on, other foodstuffs were introduced into the Mediterranean diet. This happened when the Europeans "**discovered**" America. This opened a whole new world of exotic foods. Some of the foods that were introduced from the New World include tomatoes, potatoes, chili, pepper, tomatoes, a wide variety of beans among others.

Vegetable versus Cereal

The tomato was considered an ornamental fruit initially and later became the first red vegetable before eventually becoming the symbol of the Mediterranean cuisine. While the tomato is considered one of the most crucial vegetables of this diet, then the role played by cereals cannot be overlooked.

Cereals provide the basis of simple cooking as well as a tool for day-to-day survival. Cereals helped to fill the stomachs of hungry masses and were viewed as a weapon of survival especially for the poor people. There are different types of cereals, and these are prepared differently and consumed for different purposes. Among other things, they were used to prepare soups, bread, couscous, pasta, polenta, and paella.

The similarities between the diets or foods consumed by the residents of the Mediterranean have definitely been influenced by foods from the new lands of Americans, the Muslim communities, and foods our ancestors consumed.

Nutritious Diet

The Mediterranean diet is a nutritious diet that has universal acceptance and appreciation. Consuming this diet supports all aspects of our health. It is a fact that feeding or eating has a profound effect on the health of the individual. This is basically because good nutrition helps to manage acceptable levels of health as well as prevent non-contagious diseases like hypertension or high blood pressure, cancer, diabetes, and coronary heart conditions.

American nutritionists describe the Mediterranean diet as homemade minestrone and pasta dishes of wide varieties with a sprinkling of parmesan, tomato sauce, macaroni, small fish and few pieces of meat, and freshly baked bread still hot from the oven. This diet also includes fresh fruit for dessert and lots of vegetables sprinkled with olive oil.

Diet Rich in Fiber

It is safe to conclude that the Mediterranean diet contains a wide variety of nutrients and is rich in antioxidants, fiber, and unsaturated fats. This way, it helps reduce our consumption of cholesterol and animal fats.

The Food Pyramid

There are some concepts about the Food Pyramid. One of these is proportionality. This simply means we should choose the right amount of food from each food group. The other is portion which stands for the standard quantity of food that is to be consumed.

We also have variety, and it simply implies the opportunity to choose foods from. At the bottom of the Mediterranean diet food, pyramid are grains. There is a wide variety of grains to choose from. They constitute pasta, bread, rice, grains, and potatoes. Grains are followed up the pyramid by fruits of all kinds. Fruits are vegetables are therefore an important aspect and are ranked as such. There is a wide variety to choose from so that a different variety is consumed each day.

After the fruits and vegetables on the food pyramid are the legumes, olive oil, yogurt, and low-fat cheese. These should be consumed on a daily basis without fail. While meat is included, it does not rank highly. There is a preference of poultry such as chicken and turkey or even rabbit instead of beef. Beef is basically consumed rarely, perhaps only once or twice per month.

The pyramid showcases interchangeability. This essentially implies that you have a wide variety of foods to choose from within each group. Variety is crucial for sustaining this lifestyle.

In conclusion,therefore, we can deduce that the Mediterranean diet provides a great culture for the people of the Mediterranean region and beyond especially through food. It offers an immense source of tasty, delicious recipes and foods. The people of the Mediterranean and the communities living in this region consume foods that they generally produce within their region.

It has been established by nutritionists and health scientists that eating this diet on a regular basis is bound to provide the body with all the nutrients it needs. The diet can prevent numerous diseases, especially those of the metabolic type. This diet has been touted by medics as a source of excellent health for the body. It also promotes longevity among other benefits. It finds acceptance by both patients and medics across America and numerous places all over the world.

Chapter 4: Popular Foods of the Mediterranean Diet

The food groups of the Mediterranean diet have people thinking this could be the perfect solution for anyone thinking of embarking on a healthy journey and living a healthy and sustainable lifestyle.

We have already established by now that the Mediterranean diet is rich in vegetables and fruits, whole grains, nuts and seeds, olive oil, fish, and seafood. It is low in red meat and completely free of artificial sugars and refined foods.

A Lifestyle, Not just a Diet

The Mediterranean diet offers you a lifestyle and not just a diet. If you choose this lifestyle, then you will be consuming only wholesome foods with ingredients that are excellent for your body. You will not have to be counting carbs as is the case with other diets and will not necessarily be required to eat five meals each day.

Instead, you will have to eat real food and give up most, if not all, processed foods out there. There is evidence that proves this diet is great for you. The evidence shows that this diet actually improves your health and gives you a better quality of life. Other improvements that you will experience include long-term, permanent weight loss and reduced risk of chronic illnesses.

Flavors

Apart from the healthy foods, the Mediterranean diet also features amazing flavors that are rich and sumptuous. They make the food not only tasty but also very nourishing. This is the diet that brings together tasty food that is full of flavor yet healthy and nutritious.

It is no wonder that a lot of expert tout this diet, and lifestyle, as one of the best and healthiest in the entire world. Basically, if you wish to eat foods that are great for your health and beneficial for your well being, then the following food types are highly recommended.

Here is a closer look at foods that constitute the Mediterranean diet that you should eat regularly.

1. Almonds

Almonds are great for some reasons. First, they help you lose weight and keep it off. They also taste great as nut butter, as milk, and even as a snack. They are packed with healthy oils and lots of nutrients. While they are high in fats, almonds contain the good kind of fat that is excellent for the heart. They come highly recommended because they are highly nutritious and extremely healthy.

If you work out on a regular basis, then almonds can help you lose weight faster. They also help you feel full, so you do not have to eat a lot during meal times.

Almonds are a healthy snack that you can have in the morning, afternoon or evening. They are high in proteins and also healthy, heart-friendly fats. Other nutrients found in nuts include magnesium, manganese, vitamin E, healthy fats, and fiber. Almond nuts also contain phosphorus, vitamin B2, and trace elements like copper.

Just a handful of nuts will nourish your body and pump it full of excellent nutrients. You will also get plenty of antioxidants because almonds are a fantastic source of antioxidants. Almonds are rich in Vitamin E which refers to a group of fat-soluble antioxidants. In fact, almonds are among the best source of vitamin E in the world. Studies have linked low levels of heart disease to this powerful vitamin.

2. Broccoli

Broccoli belongs to the cabbage family. It is a common Italian dark greenvegetable. It is rather bitter to the taste but packs in lots of nutrients and goodness including vitamin C, phytonutrients, carotenoids, potassium, and calcium among numerous others. This is why it is popularly referred to as a nutrition superstar and a "**super vegetable**." The fiber and carotenoids among other powerful nutrients help to keep dangerous conditions like cancer at bay. Fiber also promotes gut health and is directly linked to weight loss.

Other important and noteworthy nutrients found in broccoli include vitamin K, potassium, iron, and protein. However, what we may not be aware of is that broccoli is about 90% water with 3% protein and 7% carbs. It contains no fat and is very low in calories. One cup gives you only 31 calories, so you can consume it without worrying about weight gain.

The carbs found in broccoli are mostly sugars and fiber. The sugar is largely glucose and fructose with tiny amounts of maltose and lactose. Even then, the carbohydrate level is very low and measures about 3.5 grams per cup.

Trace elements and plant compounds found in broccoli include antioxidants, indole-3-carbinol, sulforaphane, carotenoids, and quercetin. These all assist the body fight diseases, combat inflammation, lower blood pressure, and contribute to eye health.

3. Wild Salmon

A lot of people may not be aware but swapping steak and ordering fish is actually an excellent idea. Not only is the fish absolutely delicious but is nutritious and good for your health. It is, however, advisable to choose wild salmon rather than farm-raised because the latter is usually soy fed and lack the immense benefits that wild salmons have. Research shows that salmon is one of the most nutritious foods in the world. It is loaded with nutrients and can reduce the risk factors of numerous diseases.

Salmon is delicious and popular among the residents of the Mediterranean. It is packed full of oils rich in omega-3 fatty acids. You get almost 2.5 grams in every 100 grams or 3.5 ounces of salmon. Omega-fatty acids are considered essential because they cannot be created by the body. Health experts recommend a daily intake of between 250 – 500 grams of omega-3 fatty acids that are rich in both DHA and EPA. This is equivalent to consuming 2 servings of salmon per week.

Farm raised salmons are packed rich in omega-6 fatty acids which are not good for your body. If you wish to get the best salmon, simply go down to the local fish market then ask for wild salmon. They have only 39 grams of protein per serving. Protein is an essential nutrient that should be obtained from your diet. It performs some crucial functions in the body.

4. Garlic

Garlic is largely considered a superfood because it is a powerful ingredient packed with numerous nutrients. Hippocrates, the father of modern medicine, used to prescribe garlic to treat various ailments. It is also widely used to add flavor to a wide variety of foods that are consumed in this diet. Garlic can be added to all sorts of foods including pasta and vegetables.

This little plant is capable of working with most foods well. Garlic is packed rich with vitamins such as vitamin B6 and nutrients such as manganese. It is powerful enough to rid the body of viruses, bacteria, and fungus of all kinds. A lot of these health benefits inherent in garlic have been confirmed by modern science.

Garlic's has numerous healing properties. It can combat the common cold, cure skin ailmentsregulate the heartbeat, and so much more. It also lowers your bad cholesterol levels and improves good cholesterol. This is why adding garlic to your meals is very important.

5. Chickpeas

Beans are full of goodness including nutrients such as white protein, starch, as well as calcium, folate, zinc, and iron. Chickpea is a popular legume that can be eaten regularly together with other foods. It is known by other names too such as garbanzo beans and Bengali gram. It is round and cream in color and is popular not just in Mediterranean countries but across Asia and Africa. It is sometimes combined with other grains, beans, and starches to provide a delicious yet healthy meal. It is not just healthy but also fills you up.

Chickpeas contain both insoluble and soluble fiber as well as phytosterols and phytates. Studies show that chickpea is able to assist the body fight off conditions such as diabetes, minimize heart disease risks and also prevents colon cancer. It is one of the initial grains domesticated by early man. Chickpeas were a staple food consumed regularly by ancient Egyptians, Romans, and Greeks.

Chickpeas are treasured across the Mediterranean because they are tasty and contain numerous minerals, trace elements, and other nutrients. They include healthy fats, carbohydrates, fiber, B-vitamins, potassium, calcium, molybdenum, iron, zinc, phosphorus, magnesium, and phosphorus.

6. Quinoa

One of the many ways of enjoying your quinoa is by preparing a delicious quinoa soup. Quinoa is also considered a superfood that is rich in numerous amounts of nutrients. Quinoa is naturally gluten-free and is a great source of protein. Just one cup of this amazing vegetable has about 5 grams of fiber and 8 grams of protein. It contains plenty of useful nutrients and minerals such as magnesium and calcium. Others are protein, fiber, manganese, phosphorus, folate, copper, iron, and zinc. It also contains trace minerals like phytic acid, oxalates, and quercetin.

While it has a mild flavor, it has a pleasant taste and tastes really great when cooked in foods like chicken stock or coconut milk. However, the bitter version has a lot more antioxidants compared to the sweet varieties. Even then, both serve as an excellent source for both minerals and antioxidants. In fact, quinoa has been found to have the highest antioxidant content of most cereals, legumes, and pulses.

Quinoa provides 16% protein per dry weight. It is considered by nutritionists as a complete protein source because it contains all the essential amino acids. These are important because they constitute the building blocks of all cells and tissue in our bodies. Quinoa contains a sufficient amount of fiber which is excellent for the digestive system. You get 10% fiber per dry weight of quinoa. Insoluble fiber is known for reducing your risk of diabetes while soluble fiber feeds bacteria in the gut to enhance and improve your digestive system.

7. Chia Seeds

Chia seeds are considered to be among the healthiest foods in the world. They come loaded with tons of nutrients that can do the body a lot of good. Chia seeds are the planet's greatest source of vitamin C and contain other useful nutrients including fiber, magnesium, protein, fat, manganese, calcium, vitamins, and so much more.

An ounce or 28 grams of chia seeds consists of 30% manganese, 18% calcium, 9 grams of fat that includes omega-3, 4 grams of proteins and 11 grams of fiber. Chia seeds also contain vitamin B3, Vitamin B1, potassium, zinc, and vitamin B2. This single ounce has only 137 calories with only 1 gram of carbohydrates. This is why chia seeds are considered extremely nutritious.

They will keep you satisfied and provide you with sufficient fiber for your system. There are numerous ways of consuming these seeds such as adding them to your yogurt or oatmeal and even a breakfast smoothie. Since they have almost no flavor, they will nicely blend with any food that you choose.

The benefits of chia seeds can be summarized to show that they deliver a massive amount of nutrients with very few calories. Never be deceived by the size of the seeds. While they may be tiny, they pack a powerful nutrition punch. Chia seeds are a whole grain food that is often grown organically, is free of gluten yet never genetically modified. This is why it is the world's best source for some nutrients.

8. Egg Plant

The eggplant is also known as the aubergine and is part of the nightshade family of plants. It is loved for its neutral flavor and rare texture. It is capable of blending well in sauces and introducing amazing flavors and aromas. While many consider it a vegetable, it is a fruit because it grows from a flowering plant and has seeds. There is a wide variety of eggplants with the most common being the variety with deep purple skin.

It provides meaty satisfaction to cuisines and is very popular in most Mediterranean dishes. While it does not contain as many nutrients as the superfood, it is beloved because of its effects on flavors. The eggplant is rich in nutrients that include minerals, vitamins, and trace elements.

It contains potassium and fiber as well as phytonutrients and chlorogenic acid that give it cancer-fighting and antiviral properties. It also contains protein, vitamin K, vitamin C, folate, magnesium, manganese, and carbs. Trace elements available include copper and niacin. It is, therefore, rich nutrients that are great for your body and for great health.

Eggplant is high in antioxidants. These antioxidants help protect the body from different kinds of chronic illnesses like cancer and heart disease. Eggplants are quite rich in a type of pigment known as anthocyanin. These are powerful antioxidants that your body needs. It protects against cell damage.

9. Eggs

Eggs are normally referred to as nature's multivitamin basically because they are so nutritious. They can go be consumed with most meals and have a host of benefits for your body. This means the entire egg and not just the white portion. Scientists have shown that the yolk is really the best part of the egg. It contains choline which aids in weight loss. There are numerous ways of preparing eggs including preparing delicious omelets and even baking some muffins. Eggs contain plenty of protein as well as the good cholesterol. You can find out the numerous ways of preparing eggs so that they are delicious, full of flavor as well as nutrients.

Eggs contain powerful nutrients and unique antioxidants that are essential for the brain that most people lack. Just a single egg contains sufficient nutrients to nourish a fertilized egg. These nutrients include good fats, minerals, high-quality proteins, a range of vitamins and lots of trace minerals and other less-known nutrients. These nutrients found in eggs include vitamin A, vitamins B2, B12, B5, and selenium. Other nutrients include folate, vitamin E, iron, calcium, zinc, potassium, and manganese among numerous others.

10. Ezekiel Bread

Ezekiel bread is the healthiest bread that you will ever find. This bread is a type of sprouted ancient grain bread, baked from some legumes and whole grains that have started germinating. It contains no added sugar and is a much better option than white bread and even whole grain bread as these contain processed floors and added sugars. If you have to eat bread, then always choose Ezekiel bread. It is healthier and better for you. You can find different versions of this bread some of which are flavored. A single slice of this bread has about 3 grams of fiber, yet it contains only 80 calories.

One major difference between Ezekiel bread and other types of bread is that it contains no added sugar. It is also made from sprouted, organic whole grains. The sprouting grains significantly alter the composition of the grains. Also, regular bread uses either processed wheat or pulverized whole wheat. However, Ezekiel bread consists of various legumes and cereal grains. These grains are barley, wheat, spelt, and millet while the legumes are lentils and soybeans.

11. Couscous

The base of most Mediterranean diets is usually unrefined grains such as barley, bread, couscous, and pasta. When grains remain whole and unprocessed, their glycemic index remains low. This way, they are digested slowly in the body and go through the entire system slowly and methodically.

Couscous has for a long time been a delicacy of the people living in North Africa. However, it is now an integral part of the Mediterranean diet and is consumed in many other places around the world. There are generally three different types of couscous. These are the Moroccan, Lebanese, and Israeli. They all have the same amazing benefits especially in terms of nutrition.

Selenium

Selenium is known for its anticancer properties. It helps lower your risk of cancer and also battles precursors to cancer. Scientists conducted a study that showed high selenium levels in the body to improve the body's fight against cancer. Other studies show an increase in the risk of cancers like prostate due to lower levels of selenium.

Selenium also boosts your immune system so consuming couscous is good for protecting against infections and all other manner of attacks. Couscous is also a great source of plant protein. By consuming couscous on a regular basis, your body benefits from the protein it obtains. Not only do amino acids found in proteins contribute to building the body muscle but are important in most metabolic chemical reactions.

12. Hazelnuts

In Mediterranean countries such as Italy, olive trees and nut trees are very common. This means these important food products are readily available. Nuts are generally treasured as a delicious yet healthy snack. Hazelnuts are not just consumed as nuts but are sprinkled on salads and ground into sauces. They are mostly consumed raw or roasted and are sometimes ground into a paste.

Hazelnut is packed full of vitamins, fats, and minerals. The reason why hazelnuts are so valuable in the Mediterranean diet is that they contain monounsaturated fats. These monounsaturated fats are very good for the heart. Hazelnuts contain vitamin E, fiber, magnesium, calcium, and protein. Hazelnuts are high in calories. However, they contain important nutrients. Apart from these mentioned above, hazelnuts are also rich in carbs, thiamin, copper, manganese, and healthy fats. It also contains phosphorus, folate, zinc, and potassium. It is also a rich source of crucial mono and polyunsaturated fats that contain the all-important omega-6 and omega-9 fatty acids.

13. Olive Oil

Extra virgin olive oil is regarded as the best and healthiest oil in the world. There is always the controversy about oil, especially animal fats and seed oils. People worry about their effects on our bodies. When it comes to olive oil, however, there is no controversy and no question. Extra virgin olive oil is known to be healthy oil that is good for your body and especially good for your heart.

Olive oil is especially popular when it comes to preparation of vegetables. Extra virgin olive is cold pressed directly from olives and is extremely important for cooking and dressing salads.

The extra virgin variety is rich in antioxidants and monounsaturated fats. Scientists believe that olive oil is the primary reason why residents of Mediterranean have such few incidents of heart disease. It is also believed to help ward off cancer and reduce fat in the body, especially stubborn belly fat.

14. Greek Yogurt

What is Greek yogurt? This is strained yogurt that is different from your ordinary yogurt. The producers of this beverage add an extra step during the production process. This process eliminates excess lactose, water, and minerals. The remaining product is rich, creamy, yogurt that has a tart taste, less sugar, and plenty of carbs. Your body is able to absorb the nutrients easily because of the acidity.

Yogurt is very popular among Mediterranean residents, especially Greek yogurt and Skyr. Skyr is Icelandicyogurt. Greek yogurt is prepared using goat milk. Skyr yogurt is sieved repeatedly and uses additional milk to increase the texture and flavors. The yogurts from the region use only natural ingredients such as milk from grass-fed cows, fruit, and agave. It contains none of those artificial flavors, colors, and sugars. You can sprinkle some yogurt onto your chia seeds or add a chunk to your soup.

The best way to have this yogurt is in plain form with no flavors, coloring, or artificial additives. This yogurt has numerous health benefits, and it is advisable to make it part of your regular diet. Nutrients present in this particular yogurt include proteins, probiotics, calcium, and potassium among numerous others.

15. Chicken

Chicken is one of the most popular sources of white meat today. It is also among the world's most widely consumed meats. People love chicken because it is tasty and is an excellent source of white meat. White meat is a good source of protein if you are seeking to build lean muscle, lose fat, and maintain muscle mass.

Chicken also happens to be an excellent source of protein and can form part of your diet numerous times each week. Chicken can be seared, baked, or grilled. However, you should not deep fry it. You can eat chicken till you are full. This white meat is beneficial to your body as it contains lean protein which is desirable for muscle building. You can make an entire meal based out of chicken and vegetables or combine chick with other foods like rice and so on.

16. Variety of Peppers

Mediterranean cooking involves plenty of peppers. These are used in different formats including ground and dried, fresh and even roasted. They can be ground into a variety of pastes and sauces and used to add flavor and color to different Mediterranean dishes. In addition to flavor, they also come with numerous nutrients including vitamins C and A, folate, fiber, vitamin K, beta-carotene, and lots of others. They also contain lutein, lycopene, and zeaxanthin which offer protection against conditions such as macular degeneration.

17. Shrimp

Seafood is very popular among communities living along the Mediterranean coast. One of the staple seafood that is popular among these communities is shrimp. It is among the main sources of protein and quite nutritious. Seafood such as shellfish and fish are consumed a lot because of their relative availability. These contain the crucial omega-3 fatty acids.

However, specimens such as squid and shrimp add nutrients such as niacin, protein, and selenium to the diet. Shrimp is actually a type of shellfish. Other nutrients found in shrimp include iodine, vitamin B12, phosphorus, iron, magnesium, zinc, and phosphorus. It is actually one of the best sources of iodine and is rich in antioxidants as well.

18. Tomatoes

The tomato is a fruit of the plant from the nightshade family and is native to South America. People often mistakenly think that the tomato is a vegetable. It is still hard to believe that this delicious and powerful fruit is not native to the Mediterranean. Tomatoes are a staple in every Mediterranean dish today. You will hardly come across a dish without this ubiquitous orb.

Tomatoes come in different forms including paste, canned, and fresh. They are rich in nutrients such as lycopene, carotene, bio-flavanoids and vitamin C. Lycopene is a powerful antioxidant that protects you against cancer, especially prostate cancer. Tomatoes are versatile fruits that can be added to just about any cuisine.

19. Hummus

Hummus is popularly used as a spread for your bread and as a healthy dip. It is made by blending some healthy and quality products such as garlic, olive oil, tahini, chickpeas, lemon juice, and some choice spices. Hummus is a very tasty as well as nutritious spread. The chickpeas are able to curb hunger and are loaded with useful plant protein. You can use hummus with vegetables like cucumber and celery. Some of the more popular spices used to prepare this delicious spread include sun-dried tomato, roasted red pepper, black pepper, sage, or even spice jalapeno. While it is advisable to prepare your own at home, you can also buy hummus brands at the grocery store.

20. Cauliflower

Cauliflower is one of the most popular vegetables in the Mediterranean diet. It is an extremely healthy vegetable that can nourish the body and keep it in excellent health. It contains essential plant compounds that can reduce the risk of diseases like cancer and heart disease.

Cauliflower is used to prepare most dishes and is a useful ingredient because of the amazing flavor and great taste that it brings. It is also packed full of minerals and nutrients that are great for your health. It is great for weight loss and is easy to include in your regular diet.

Chapter 5: Benefits of the Mediterranean Diet

The Mediterranean diet has been touted as one of the world's best diets and lifestyles. The diet has been scientifically proven to be beneficial in numerous ways. This is mostly due to its emphasis on whole grains, high fiber intake, antioxidants, healthy fats, fish, fresh produce and moderate intake of red meat and alcohol.

By following this lifestyle, you will enjoy most meals with your family or loved ones as you can prepare most meals at home. Cooking together as a family and enjoying a glass of red wine afterward is the kind of lifestyle envisioned by the Mediterranean diet. This diet expects you to consume plenty of fresh produce that is non-starchy. You should aim for about 5 small meals throughout the day that include not just fresh produce but also some healthy oils. These oils can be from avocado, fish, nuts, or olive oil. Your meals should also include lots of fish, eggs, and dairy protein such as yogurt or cheese.

Health Benefits of the Mediterranean Diet

The Mediterranean diet is considered an ideal diet because you do not have to go to any extremes. You are able to enjoy a great quality of life and enjoy delicious, well-prepared foods that you and your loved ones will enjoy. You are allowed to eat regularly without skipping meals and so on. Once you begin living this lifestyle, you will shortly thereafter notice a lot of difference in your life. You should expect to notice a difference in your brain, heart health, and longevity.

1. The Mediterranean Diet Keeps You Agile with Age

The meals that you consume with your Mediterranean diet contain a lot of useful minerals, vitamins, essential oils, and numerous other nutrients. Because of all these nutrients, you should expect to benefit in various ways. For instance, you will have a lower risk of conditions such as fragility and muscle weakness.

Senior citizens who follow this diet have shown rapid improvement in their health with stronger bones and more muscle than their peers. Their risk for such conditions can be reduced by up to 70% by simply switching to this diet. If you want to lead this lifestyle successfully into your later years, begin by eating plenty of fresh vegetables, fruits, lean proteins and healthy fats. These will keep your muscles supple and lean, your bones strong and your body agile.

2. This Diet is Excellent for a Healthy Heart

Heart and coronary conditions are much lower across the Mediterranean than in the United States and other parts of the world. This can be directly attributed to diet choices of the communities living around the Mediterranean. According to experts, the healthy oils from nuts, salmon, and olives are great for the heart. They promote heart health and circulation.

Dietary choices also enhance good heart health. Remember that it is not just the food that you eat that matters but also what you drink. The Mediterranean diet also promotes an active lifestyle. It encourages physical activity as well as social support. A glass of wine taken occasionally and lots of healthy juices will support a healthy body and a healthy heart. Red wine has been linked to lower heart disease risks. However, you should limit your intake to about one or two glasses per day.

Moderation is a key to a healthy body. A good aspect to focus on is bad cholesterol. The Mediterranean diet promotes healthy oils that are great for the heart. It also helps to eliminate bad cholesterol that is often deposited in the arteries and causes cardiovascular problems.

3. It Protects against Type II Diabetes

Type II diabetes occurs when there is unregulated sugar in the blood. This often caused by excessive consumption of processed starch and high glycemic carbs. The Mediterranean diet has proven to be a lot more effective than all other diets in protecting against diabetes.

Scientists compared the Mediterranean diet against other diets that include vegan, vegetarian, high protein, high fiber, and numerous others. The results show that the Mediterranean diet is much more effective at combating diabetes compared to all others. Research scientists placed an emphasis on foods containing monounsaturated oils such as olive oil, fish such as salmon, vegetables, and fruits. These have been shown to lower cholesterol and blood sugar levels in people suffering from diabetes.

4. The Diet Reduces Chances of Developing Alzheimer's Disease

The Mediterranean diet includes foods that improve blood sugar, lower cholesterol and the overall health of your cardiovascular system. All these benefits work together and reduce your risks or chances of suffering from conditions like Alzheimer's.

There is research-based evidence that shows the Mediterranean diet helps protect against conditions like cognitive decline. This way, adults, especially seniors are able to limit the burden of illness and preserve or maintain their quality of life. Doctors advise patients to lead healthier lifestyles such as adopting the Mediterranean diet. Healthy eating habits, regular exercises, and keeping busy throughout the day all help in addressing conditions like dementia and similar cognitive conditions.

5. Lose Weight the Healthy Way

A lot of overweight and obese people struggle to lose weight. This is often because they do this the wrong way. Many opt for diets that are temporary or do not work. It is important to change lifestyle completely to enjoy the benefits inherent to the chosen lifestyle.

Losing weight through the Mediterranean diet comes in some ways. None of the recommended food items is actually fattening. All the carbs are low glycemic which means they are digested slowly and keep you feeling full longer. They do not contain any processed carbohydrates or starches or unhealthy oils.

To lose significant weight healthily, you should also lead an active lifestyle. For instance, you can engage in regular exercises on a regular basis. Alternatively, you can take deliberate steps to be active such as using the stairs often and walking to the grocery store. Finally, maintain your portions with every meal. You should not overeat because this is often the main cause of obesity.

6. Mediterranean Diet Helps Fight Cancer

Research scientists have proven that the Mediterranean diet can help fight against cancer. It has clearly demonstrated that a proper eating plan based on this diet can actually lead to reduced risk of cancer as well as cancer-related deaths. The foods that constitute the Mediterranean diet such as olive oil, eggs, salmon, and others contain numerous nutrients including trace elements, selenium, antioxidants, omega-3 fatty acids and many more.

All these nutrients work together to eliminate toxins in the body and remove waste from the cells. Antioxidants are effective in combating free radicals most of which are thought to be a prelude to cancer. Mediterranean diet plays a major role in the prevention of cancer. This lifestyle, in particular, helps to prevent the development of radical cancers such as postmenopausal breast cancer.

7. It Enhances Relaxation

When you adopt the Mediterranean lifestyle, you should also adopt other aspects to fully benefit from it. This means spending more time with your family, cooking and eating together and engaging in other families as well. By spending quality time with people that you have, you will relax your mind and enhance the release of the feel-good hormone.

These hormones such as serotonin calm you down and help you to relax. Calming your nerves and heart enhances overall health and promote longevity. Basically, eating nutritious meals and relaxing your mind and body gives you a more relaxed lifestyle.

8. The Mediterranean Diet Helps Fight Inflammation in the Body

Inflammation occurs within the body. When this happens, you are at risk of various major illnesses and your health will be compromised. The good news is that the Mediterranean diet helps reduce inflammation in the body. Studies have indicated a reduction in intensity of inflammation markers in high-risk individuals.

Inflammation is often caused by exposure to oxidative stress. The antioxidants contained in the Mediterranean diet are able to combat oxidative stress successfully. You can improve this action by eating more foods that contain choline such as soybeans and egg yolks as well as spinach and beetroots.

9. This Diet is Excellent for your Skin

The Mediterranean diet is excellent for your skin. The skin is a crucial organ that serves numerous purposes like protecting other organs and eliminating waste. If you consume plenty of vegetables and fruit, foods rich in antioxidants, olive oil and lots of water, then you will soon love the look of your skin.

Tomatoes protect the skin against free radicals and even against skin cancers due to sun exposure. Red wine in moderation is also a part of the Mediterranean diet. It contains antioxidants that are useful for the skin.

10. Mediterranean Diet Halves your Chances of Suffering Parkinson's Disease

Parkinson's disease is a debilitating disease that affects quality of life in later years. Fortunately, the Mediterranean diet provides you with sufficient amounts of antioxidants. The levels of antioxidants in this diet will help you cut your risks by half. These are found mostly in the healthy fats, seafood dishes, vegetables, and fruits that you eat.

The antioxidants protect your cells from exposure to oxidative stress. Oxidative stress damages cells and this can result in the development of debilitating diseases like Parkinson's.

11. It Protects Cognitive Health

The Mediterranean diet will help improve your cognitive ability. Scientists have proven that individuals who follow this diet have superior focus and attention as well as enhanced memory. The diet also enhances the brain's language capabilities. This is important for those who wish to maintain brain function throughout life as well as fending off dementia in elderly persons. You will experience a considerable enhanced quality of life even in your old age.

12. Mediterranean Diet Helps Improve Mood

This diet, and associated lifestyle, offers plenty of brain promoting benefits. People suffering mental health challenges such as ADHD, depression, and anxiety will definitely benefit from the Mediterranean diet.

The issues of anxiety and other mental health conditions usually occur due to dopamine deficiency. Dopamine is the enzyme responsible for mood regulation. Following this diet regularly will enable your body produce this chemical and keep your brain happy and mood elevated.

13. It Can Help with Pain Relief

Whole grains and fiber rich foods that are common in the Mediterranean region are rich in nutrients such as magnesium. Fresh fruits and green leafy vegetables can also contribute to your pain management plan. Such a diet can also help you reduce dependence on pain killers. Your body will respond to pain differently because the diet also combats inflammation and helps minimize stress levels. It is very possible that your chronic pain could disappear thanks to the Mediterranean diet.

Chapter 6: Meal Plans for A Week

The Mediterranean lifestyle requires that you eat specific types of foods. The diet is typically high in healthy plant food but low in animal foods. Even then, seafood and fish are highly recommended. Drink plenty of water, fruit and vegetable juices, and red wine. Tea and coffee are also allowed, but beverages with high levels of added sugars are not allowed.

This diet is basically focused on legumes, tubers, nuts and seeds, fruits, vegetables, whole grains, herbs and spices, poultry, dairy, eggs, and healthy fats. Experts believe that whole, single-ingredient foods are the key to excellent health.

Sample Menu for a Week

Here is a sample menu based on the Mediterranean lifestyle. Please keep in mind that nutritionists and health experts insist that there is no need to track macronutrients or count calories on the Mediterranean diet. You also don't need to eat more than three times per day, but snacking in-between meals is allowed.

Monday

- Breakfast: Oats with milk, Greek yogurt with strawberries
- Lunch: wholegrain chicken sandwich, tomatoes, onions and veggie salad
- Dinner: Tuna fish salad with olive oil and a succulent fruit

Tuesday

- Breakfast: Nuts and sliced fruits with yogurt
- Lunch: Mediterranean lasagna
- Dinner: Pan fried salmon served with vegetables and brown rice

Wednesday

- Breakfast: Tropical fruit and omelet with tomatoes, onions, and veggies

- Lunch: Wholegrain sandwich with fresh vegetables and cheese
- Dinner: Mediterranean lasagna left over from the previous day

Thursday

- Breakfast: raisins and oatmeal with fruits and nuts
- Lunch: leftover lasagna from the previous night
- Dinner: Vegetable salad with olives, tomatoes, and feta cheese

Friday

- Breakfast: veggies, omelet, and olives
- Lunch: wholegrain rice with cowpeas stew
- Dinner: roast potatoes, grilled chicken, vegetables, and fruit

Saturday

- Breakfast: vegetables and eggs pan fried with olive oil

- Lunch: Greek yogurt and strawberries, nuts and oats
- Dinner: Baked potato, a salad, and grilled lamb

Sunday

- Raisins and oatmeal with hazelnuts and a fruit
- Whole grain turkey sandwich with vegetables
- Lasagna with cheese, olives, and vegetables

Healthy Snacks to Accompany your Meals

Sometimes you may feel hungry during the day. Alternatively, you may wish to have a snack in the day or evening. You could always choose to have a snack. The Mediterranean lifestyle offers a wide variety of healthy snacks that are good for your health. Feel free to choose from one of these.

- Some grapes and berries

- Carrots
- A piece of fruit
- A handful of nuts or seeds
- Apple slices
- Greek yogurt

Simple Mediterranean Dishes you can Prepare at Home

1. Greek Fish Stew

This is a Greek cuisine that serves two to four people. It takes 5 minutes to prepare and about 30 minutes to cook.

Ingredients

- 1 ¼ cups of sliced and diced onions
- 4 cod fillets

- ¼ cup olive oil
- 1 cup of water
- 1 teaspoon of pepper
- 1 teaspoon of salt
- ¼ teaspoon each cayenne and paprika

Instructions

Add water to a pan and put it on the stove with medium heat. Then pour in the olive oil as well as the onions, cayenne, pepper, salt, and paprika. Let the mixture boil then reduce the heat. Allow it to simmer for a couple of minutes until the onions soften.

Now add the fish slices to the stew and let it continue simmering for about 5 to 10 minutes. Check to see if the fish is cooked and remove from the stove. If it is ready, serve on dishes with the onion mixture.

2. The Fattoush Salad

The Fattoush salad is a simple bread salad that is popular throughout North Africa and southern Europe. It consists of chopped salad dressed with line vinaigrette. It can be enjoyed with some pita chips. Ingredients do vary from one location to another, but the idea is the same.

Ingredients

- Cucumbers
- Tomatoes
- Lettuce leaves
- Green onions
- Radish
- Fresh herbs such as mint or parsley
- 2 loaves pita bread
- Salt and pepper
- Extra virgin olive

Preparation

Chop the vegetables and slice or dice the herbs to suit your needs. Make sure you always select the best produce at the grocery store. Prepare your own pita chips at home rather than buy at the store. Slice the pita bread and toast it to a crisp brown color.

Add the herbs to the chopped vegetables then pour in your extra virgin olive oils. If you can, always use the extra virgin olive oil. Other olive oils may not be pure simple because the extraction methods may have affected the purity and effectiveness. You can top up the dish with vinaigrette and even molasses if you like.

3. Chicory and Beans

This is a common dish across the Mediterranean. Inhabitants prefer eating their vegetables, pasta, and lentils during the week saving their meats for the weekends. The following dish serves 4 to 6 people and is of Italian background.

Ingredients

- 1 can of well rinsed and drained beans
- 2 to 3 medium heads of chicory
- 3 cloves of garlic
- 1 tablespoon of Olive oil
- ½ teaspoon of salt

Preparation

Soak your chicory in water then repeat this several times until it is clean then chop off the roots. Now boil the chicory in hot, salted water for about 10 minutes or until tender. Once it is tender, drain and reserves the water.

Take a large sauté pan and place on the stove with low heat. Pour in some olive oil and add the garlic. Let it brown then add red pepper. Remove the pan from the heat after a few minutes.

Now add the chicory to the seasoned oil and let the mixture simmer for 5 to 10 minutes. Add the boiled beans and the reserved (drained) water. Mix well and take care not to damage the beans.

4. Lemon Shrimp Pasta

This is a popular and delicious Italian dish that is easy to prepare and great for the whole family. Here is how to prepare the lemon shrimp pasta.

Ingredients

- 1 pound of shrimp
- 1 large red onion
- 4 cloves of garlic
- ½ cup of white wine
- 1 cup of chicken broth
- ½ tablespoon red hot chili pepper powder
- 1 lemon squeezed

Preparation

Take out the shrimp and thaw it out. Now slice the onion and dice the garlic then sauté them on a pan for just a couple of minutes. Toss in the shrimp and let it cook for a few minutes then pour in the white wine. Add the red-hot chili pepper and the lemon juice and allow it to cook for a few minutes.

Once it is cooked, let it simmer, so the shrimp is poached. Meanwhile, you could prepare the pasta at the same time. Once the pasta is boiled, you take it out and add to the skillet with the shrimp and sauce. You can add some chopped parsley and grated parmesan cheese.

5. Marinated Cod and Cabbage

Ingredients

- 6 cups of seafood broth
- ½ pound of codfish
- 1 dozen mussels
- 12 large shrimps
- 1 tablespoon sea salt
- 2 tablespoons of minced parsley
- 8 cloves of diced garlic
- 2 teaspoons of paprika
- 1 medium-sized, chopped onion
- 1 large, chopped tomato
- 1 diced red bell pepper

- Lemon wedges

Preparation

Prepare and heat the broth in a large pot. Add the fish and shrimp then sprinkle some salt and allow to simmer for 10 minutes. Mash some thyme, garlic, and parsley then add some salt and add to the mixture. Add water and pour in the paprika.

Put a pan on fire then add some olive oil. Once hot, add the shrimp and fish until brown. Add the bell pepper and onions then cook till the vegetables become soft. Now raise the heat and pour in the broth. Pour in the rice evenly and allow it to boil till ready or for three minutes. Now arrange the clams, shrimp, and mussels on top of the rice. Let the food sit on the heat for a couple of minutes so the rice cooks. You can then garnish the food with lemon wedges.

6. Chickpeas and Eggplant Salad

Ingredients

- 1 garlic clove skinned and bashed
- 1 large eggplant chopped up into cubes
- 1 can of well-drained chickpeas
- 1 teaspoon of paprika
- 4 tablespoons of extra virgin olive oil
- Pepper and sea salt for seasoning
- Parsley leaves

Preparation

Take a large sauté pan and heat the olive oil. Pour in the mashed garlic and heat till brown. Add the eggplant then stir well till it is well coated with the oil. Reduce heat and let it steam so that the vegetables cook slowly for about 15 minutes. Keep stirring occasionally till cooked.

Once the eggplant is cooked and turns a nice brown color, pour in the paprika and chickpeas, then stir well and let it simmer. Add salt and pepper to taste then simmer for a couple more minutes then serve.

7. Greek Style Zucchini Blossoms with Bulgur

Ingredients

- 3 cloves of garlic
- ½ teaspoon each of pepper and sea salt
- 1 teaspoon of chili pepper
- 1 cup of olive oil
- 1 cup each, chopped onion and chives
- 1 cup of grated zucchini
- 25 zucchini blossoms

- 3 cups of yogurt
- 2/3 cups of raisins
- ½ cup of water

Preparation

Take a deep skillet and pour in about half of the olive oil. Put on the stove on medium heat and sauté the garlic, chives, and onion for 5 minutes. Now add the chili pepper, raisins, bulgur, and zucchini. Then pour in the water and reduce the heat, so the mixture simmers for 10 minutes.

Now turn off the stove then add the mint and pine nuts to the stuffing. Add salt and pepper for seasoning. Use a spoon to stuff each blossom carefully and fold the sides together. Pour in the rest of the olive oil and ½ cup of water. Bake for about 1 hour or until most of the liquid has been absorbed. Serve hot or cold and throw in yogurt if possible.

8. Parsley Salad with Cucumber, Bulgur, and Tomatoes

This is a simple dish with very few ingredients. Always opt for the best and freshest ingredients in the market. Here is a closer look at this dish.

Ingredients

- 1 cup fresh parsley
- 2 tablespoons olive oil
- 1 large red tomato
- ½ cup of tender cucumber
- ½ tablespoon each of salt and pepper

Procedure

Prepare the dressing by chopping up all the vegetables then dicing them into a bowl. Soak the bulgur in the dressing so that it absorbs the flavors. Dice the parsley and add it as a dressing. This mixture can be garnished with herbs such as garlic and others.

9. Homemade Hummus

Humus is a delicious dip and can be used as a side sauce. While there are numerous commercial ones available at grocery stores, it is advisable to prepare your own at home and enjoy it with your favorite dish.

Ingredients

- 400 grams chickpeas
- 1 large lemon juiced
- 3 tablespoons tahini
- ¼ cup of water
- A pinch of paprika
- ½ teaspoon ground cumin
- 2 cloves of minced garlic
- 4 tablespoons of extra virgin olive oil

Directions

Mix lemon juice and tahini in a blender for 1 minute. Add the chickpeas to the blender and mix till completely minced. Now add the olive oil and minced garlic and continue mixing. Blend until the oil is completely soaked in. Add seasoning including cumin and salt then pour 2 tablespoons of water. Let this mixture blend in the machine for one more minute. Add a bit more water if the mixture is too thick.

10. Chicken Tagine with Almonds, Chickpeas, and Apricots

Tagine is the name for both the North African dish and *the vessel in which it's prepared*. The idea is very similar to Western-style braising in Dutch ovens: combine ingredients, cover, and cook over low heat until tender and tasty. The tagine traps steam, creating a very moist cooking environment with even heat.

Ingredients

- 1 teaspoon coriander
- 2 cloves of minced garlic

- 1-inch piece of ginger peeled and minced
- 1 teaspoon of cumin
- 1 carrot peeled and diced
- 1 teaspoon cinnamon
- 1 yellow onion sliced and diced
- 3 pounds of chicken thighs and legs
- 1 cup of dried couscous
- 1 tablespoon honey
- ½ cup of dried and chopped apricots
- ½ cup of dried and chopped almonds

Directions

Warm a tablespoon of oil in an oven over medium heat till the oil is shimmering. Sprinkle salt and pepper on the chicken pieces and place as many pieces as possible. Let this sear for a couple of minutes, 5 – 8 to be precise, flipping occasionally until both sides turn a nice golden brown.

Remove all the chicken pieces to a bowl then put the pan back on the stove with medium heat. Add some olive oil then sauté some carrots and onions. Season these with salt and pepper. Stir until soft then add the garlic. Cook for about 30 seconds and then sprinkle the spices and ginger into the mix.

Add the chicken pieces and apricot into the pan and reduce the heat to low. Bring this mixture to a boil with low heat. While the chicken is cooking, prepare the couscous on the side. Once the chicken is ready, pour it onto a plate. Put the pan back onto the stove and add the chickpeas, almonds, onions, and honey. Add salt and pepper to the stew if necessary.

11. Salmon with Cabbage and Garlic Sandwich

This is a perfect meal for either lunch or dinner. This delicious fish dish is of Greek origin but is now popular around the world. You will enjoy a mild taste of delicious cod with creamy texture and tangy flavors in a soft, toasted sub roll. Here is a simple recipe that you can prepare at home.

Ingredients

- 1 cup of Mojo juice

- ¼ cup olive oil
- 1 head of cabbage diced
- ½ teaspoon of minced garlic
- Brown rolls
- 4 fresh salmon fillets

Mustard Sauce

- 3 teaspoons of Dry Mustard
- 2 teaspoons of Worcester sauce
- Pinch of salt
- 2 tablespoons of whipping cream
- 1 cup of mayo

Procedure

Start by marinating the fish in mojo sauce for about one hour. Next ensure that the cabbaged is nicely chopped and diced to fine slices then set aside. Now mix all the ingredients for the mustard sauce in a small bowl. Refrigerate the bowl with all its contents until required.

After an hour's soaking, the fish fillet should be ready. Put the skillet on the stove and pour in the olive oil. Put the fish fillet in the skillet and add the seasoning. Let it cook until it turns a nice golden-brown color on each side.

Take another skillet then sauté the cabbage with garlic and olive oil. Sauté the cabbage until the cabbage softens, now slice the freshly baked brown toasted slices and spread the sauce evenly on both sides. Place a slice of fish in each and then top it with sautéed cabbage.

12. Chorizo, Mushroom, and Haloumi Tacos

Mushroom, chorizo, and haloumi tacos constitute the tantalizing trio. You can make this dish for a nice summer lunch or even dinner. Tacos are not originally Mediterranean, but haloumi is. This dish takes 20 minutes for preparations and 40 minutes cook time.

Ingredients

- Freshly chopped chilies
- ½ kilo button mushrooms, clean and cut into quarters
- 1 teaspoon salt
- 1 teaspoon black pepper
- 3 tablespoons olive oil
- Chopped coriander
- 8 medium size warm tortillas
- 1 large, cooked sausage sliced into nice chunks
- 200 grams haloumi cheese sliced into two
- A pinch of dried Greek oregano

Preparation

Put the mushroom in a bowl and add the olive oil. Now sprinkle the oregano, sea salt, and pepper. Mix all the ingredients thoroughly and then place on a baking tray. Put this in the oven at 200 degrees C for half an hour then remove from oven and allow it to cool.

Take a pan and pre-heat some olive oil on medium heat. Cook the chorizo for a couple of minutes until it turns crispy then remove it and set aside. Using the same pan fry the haloumi on both side until nice and soft. When ready, remove from the pan and cut into smaller pieces.

Take a spate bowl and use it to combine the chorizo, mushrooms, and haloumi. If you wish to make some tacos, place about 4 tablespoons of mushroom mixture in a hot tortilla. Garnish with coriander and fresh chilies then serve instantly.

13. Louvi – Black Eyed Beans with Chard

Louvi is the name given to black eyed beans in Cyprus. They are perfect for any meal and can be either part of the main meal or side dish. It takes 15 minutes to prepare Louvi and about one hour of cooking time.

Ingredients

- 250 grams of black-eyed beans
- 1 medium sized onion finely diced
- 3 cups or 1 bunch of chard (Silver beet)
- 1 clove of garlic finely chopped
- 1 spring onion diced
- ¼ cup of olive oil
- A pinch of salt
- 2 to 3 tablespoons of finely chopped parsley
- 1 tablespoon of fennel fronds
- 4 cups of water
- ½ cup of lemon juice

Directions

Boil the clack eyed beans in a pot of water for about 15 to 20 minutes. At the same time, was the silver beet and then cut it up into smaller pieces. Take a pan and sauté the garlic and onion with extra virgin olive oil. Add the silver beet and stir.

Now pour the beans into the saucepan and add some salt and pepper. Add some water and lemon juice then cover the saucepan. Let the mixture simmer until it finally boils. Lower heat and let the beans cook on low heat. Remove once the black-eyed beans are soft.

Turn off the heat once the beans get soft then mix in the dill and parsley. The food is now ready to serve so serve with lemon juice and a little bit of olive oil.

14. Braised Okra

Braised okra is a popular Greek dish and a tasty vegetarian dish. It is also very easy to prepare especially because it contains very few ingredients. Okra dishes are almost always vegetarian and include tomatoes and garlic. Using olive oil to braise vegetables this way gives them an additional taste.

Ingredients

- 2 tablespoons red wine vinegar
- ½ kilo fresh okra
- 1 finely chopped onion
- ½ cup of olive oil
- A handful of freshly chopped, flat leaf parsley

- 500 grams of fresh pureed tomatoes
- Salt and pepper to taste

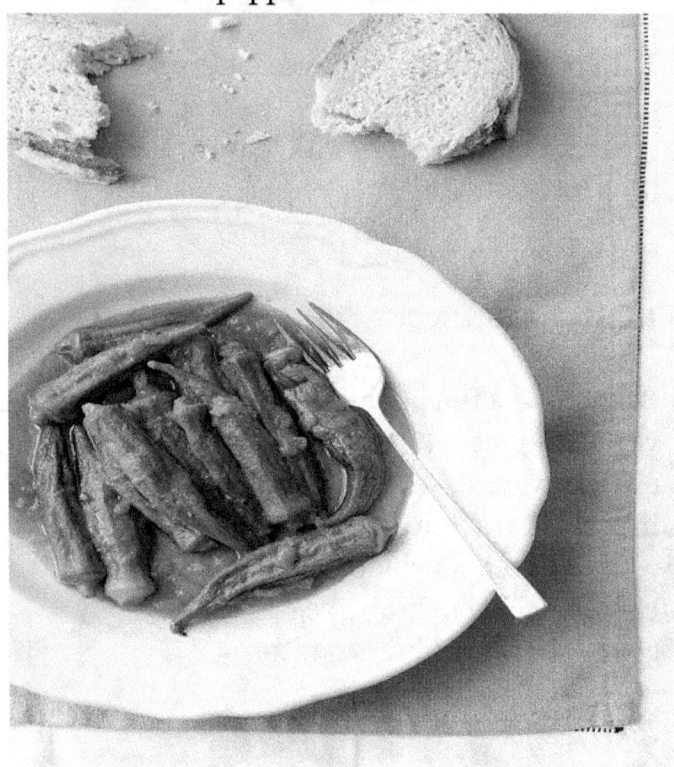

How to Prepare

First clean the okra using water then trim off the pointy ends. Next take the red wine vinegar and sprinkle it on the okra then let it sit for about an hour. After the hour is over, rinse the okra in cold water and then drain.

Take a heavy bottomed sauce pan then heat some olive oil. Sauté the onion on low heat until it turns a nice brown color and soft texture. Once the onions become soft, you should add the okras and the olive oil then let this cook for about five minutes.

Add the parsley and tomatoes then season with pepper and salt to taste. Let this mixture sit on the fire for a short while until it boils. It should boil at possibly 20 to 30 minutes. Once the okra is ready, you should take it off the fire and serve it straight away whilst still hot. Serve with crusty, freshly baked bread.

15. Kale and Lentil Soup

This is a sumptuous recipe that makes use of kale. Kale can be switched with spinach or Swiss chard. Ensure that the vegetables and ingredients are fresh. Here is how to prepare the recipe.

Ingredients

- 3 carrots diced
- 1 onion diced
- 3 celery ribs, sliced
- 1 bay leaf
- 3 garlic cloves diced
- 1/3 cup of flat leaf parsley leaves
- 1 tablespoon of fresh thyme leaves
- 32 ounces of low salt chicken or vegetable broth
- ½ bunch of kale, stemmed, chopped, and rinsed
- 1 cup equivalent to ½ pound of lentils, sorted and rinsed

Preparation method

Take all the ingredients, except for the kale, and mix them in a large pot. Put the pot on a stove on medium to high heat, then cover and leave to boil. Once the mixture boils, stir it for a while then add kale leaves and continue stirring. Continue cooking until the kale wilts and carrots and lentils are tender. This should take a further 10 minutes.

Now puree the soup using an immersion blender. Once the blend is complete, refrigerate in an airtight container for as long as you want. You can also serve it immediately for lunch or dinner.

16. Grilled Fish in Saffron Sauce

Grilled fish is a delightful dish that is pretty easy to make. Grilled fish in Saffron Sauce is of Lebanese origin. You will need whole fish for this recipe. However, if you do not like staring at a fish, then you can find alternatives, like swordfish. It takes 5 minutes to prepare the fish, 10 minutes of cooking time and a further 10 passive minutes.

Ingredients

- 4 fishes, any species common along the Mediterranean area
- 1 pinch of saffron
- ½ cup of olive oil or walnut oil
  1 teaspoon of sea salt
- 1 large lemon or lime sliced into 4 pieces

- ½ cup of tomato sauce or 1 tablespoon of ketchup or tomato paste
- ½ teaspoon of white pepper can be substituted with sumac or cumin

Instructions

Heat your grill oven until it is very hot. As it heats up, season the fish and then brush with oil. Also brush the grill with oil to prevent the fish from sticking. Now put the fish in the grill and leave it there for 3 minutes for each side.

Mix in a small bowl the ingredients of the sauce. Add tomato sauce or paste in order to improve the taste. Brush the fish with the tomato sauce occasionally. Once the fish is nice and crispy, it is ready to eat. Serve whilst hot with lime or lemon quarters.

17. Barbunya Pilaki – Cranberry Beans Cooked with Vegetables

Barbunya Pilaki is a typical Turkish meal that can be served cold as a side dish, or hot as the main dish. Among other things, this meal contains cranberry beans which are known as Borlotti along the Mediterranean.

The beans are cooked in olive oil with carrots, onions, and tomatoes. Pilaki is a Turkish cooking style that means cooking vegetables and beans are cooked with tomato, garlic, and onions on a pan with olive oil.

Ingredients

- 2 cups of dried cranberry (Borlotti) beans soaked overnight in warm water
- 1 finely chopped medium or large onion
- Freshly ground black pepper and salt
- 1 whole lemon split into wedges

- 2 cups of water
- Three tablespoons of olive oil
- A handful of finely chopped flat leaf parsley
- 2 teaspoons of sugar
- 1 can of quality tomatoes chopped
- 2 medium size carrots chopped into small boxes

Procedure

Soak the dried cranberry beans overnight for about 8 hours. Drain the beans the following day, then rinse and put in a container filled with cold water. Put this pot on the stove and bring to a boil.

Now rinse and drain the beans that are already cooled. Set these aside. Take the olive oil and heat it then sauté the onions. Sauté until the color turns brown or onions become soft. Pour in the carrots and sauté for a further two minutes. Season with salt and add some sugar, tomatoes and freshly ground black pepper.

Now let this sauté for about 2 minutes while stirring occasionally. Then add the beans to the pot and mix it thoroughly. Add some water to the mix and then bring it to a boil. Let it simmer on low heat for about half an hour and check the seasoning. Serve whilst hot as the main dish or cold as a side dish.

18. Eggplant Frittata

A frittata is a popular Italian egg-based dish almost similar to an omelet or scrambled eggs. Frittatas are the epitome of summer from the sweet aroma to savory flavors. They constitute a healthy non-meat meal. You can use eggplant to make a frittata. Here is the procedure.

Ingredients

- 700 grams of eggplants peeled and cubed
- 8 free range eggs
- 1 large onion diced
- A tablespoon of chopped parsley
- 2 ounces of grated cheese
- 6 cloves of garlic crushed
- 2 tablespoons of extra virgin olive oil
- Salt and pepper to taste

Procedure

Put the eggplant cubes on a plate and sprinkle some sea salt. Let them sit there for a while. After about 30 minutes, rinse them and pat them dry using paper towels. Take a skillet, add the olive oil and put it on the stove.

Sauté the onion then add the garlic and eggplant cubes. Cook these on medium heat until they turn a nice golden color. Keep stirring them regularly. Take a bowl and whisk the eggs then add the cheese and season with salt and pepper.

Now pour the egg and cheese mixture to the skillet with the cooked eggplants. Pour such that the egg mixture goes to the bottom of the skillet. Cover the skillet and cook on low heat until it is all cooked. Take the chopped parsley and sprinkle on top then serve.

19. Calamari Salad

Calamari salad features crisp bell peppers, tender calamari, and zesty lemon dressing. It is fresh, light, healthy and delicious. While you can eat it right away and it is absolutely delicious, letting it sit for a while to allow the flavors to develop is a better idea.

Ingredients

- 1 Thinly sliced red onion
- 1 Pound of fresh squid rings
- 1 Minced garlic clove
- ½ Pound of mixed baby salad leaves

- ½ Cup of Kalamata olives, halved along the length
- 2 Cups of cherry tomatoes sliced into halves
- 1/3 Cup of extra virgin olive oil
- A splash of red wine vinegar
- 2 tablespoons of freshly squeezed lemon juice
- Freshly ground pepper and salt
- ½ Cup of water

Preparations

Take a bowl and whisk vinegar, lemon juice, garlic, and oil. Add some pepper and salt and stir. Add the onion, stir some more, and then set aside. Take the squid rinks and rinse thoroughly. Boil salted water in an oven then add the squid rings. Cook the squid in the oven, uncovered, for about a minute. Drain in a colander and then put under cold running water for about a minute. Once the squid has cooled, pat it down using paper towels.

Take a large bowl and add salad leaves together with tomatoes and olives. Now add the squid to the salad. Pour in the dressing and mix thoroughly. Check the seasoning and confirm if it is adequate then add some if necessary. If you let the salad sit for a couple of minutes, the flavors will blend nicely, making it even juicier and tastier.

20. Sautéed Greens with Tomatoes and Onions

This is a simple yet perfect recipe for winter. It is popularly known as Tsigareli which is Greek for cabbage with red spicy peppers, fresh tomato, and herbs such as parsley and dill. Here is the preparation process.

Ingredients

- 2.5 Pounds fresh, mixed, and tender greens like dandelion and spinach
- 2 Large onions sliced and diced
- 2 Minced garlic cloves
- ¼ Cup of extra virgin olive oil
- 1.5 Cups of mint leaves or wild fennel leaves
- 2 Leeks washed and finely diced
- 1.5 Cups of snipped fresh dill
- 1 Cup of peel and finely chopped tomatoes
- 2 Teaspoons of sweet paprika powder
- Pepper and salt to taste
- 2 Tablespoons tomato paste
- 1 Teaspoon cayenne pepper

Process

Take the greens and blanch until wilted then drain them thoroughly. Now take a large skillet and heat the olive oil in medium heat. Add the onions and leek and cook until soft, stirring regularly. This should take between 5 to 7 minutes.

Add the cayenne, tomato paste, paprika, and garlic then stir for a couple of minutes. Add the wild fennel leaves, dill, and wilted greens and the tomatoes. Stir for 3 minutes then let it simmer uncovered for about 20 minutes on low heat or until the greens are soft.

By now the dish should be dry so check the seasoning and add salt and cayenne pepper if necessary. The dish is now ready for serving so serve whilst still hot with fresh bread. You can pour some olive oil on the greens once cooked.

Weight Loss and Diet Plan

The Mediterranean diet is more of a lifestyle than a diet. It involves eating nuts and other foods that contain healthy monounsaturated fats. These are good for the heart and keep you feeling fuller. This way, you will eat less and lose weight. When you consume your food, you get most of your nutrition from fiber-rich whole grains like quinoa, barley, oats and brown rice. These foods are natural and non-fattening. They are easily eliminated from the body.

This diet focuses more on fish and seafood and less on red meat. Fish has heart-friendly oils like omega-3 fatty acids. Get rid of red meats and go for tuna, salmon, and sardines. Use olive oil a lot, especially the extra virgin type. This oil is good for your body and has numerous benefits. Add spices and herbs to keep calories down and improve on taste. You do not have to give up on red meat altogether. However, you can have red meat once or twice each month with your meals.

Eat roughly 2000 to 2500 calories of food per day. Half your plate should always consist of a mixture of vegetables. The other half is divided equally so that one side has your protein and the other your carbs. Keeping your portions small and calories low will enable you to lose weight and keep it off.

Conclusion

Thank you for making it through to the end of this book, let's hope it was informative and has provided you with all of the tools you need to achieve your goals whatever they may be.

The next step is to start following this lifestyle. You should come up with your own plan to see how best to implement the Mediterranean diet. It offers a great pathway to healthy eating, great health, weight loss, lower stress, family time, and so much more.

Experts have claimed that this is the best diet and healthiest lifestyle in the world. If you can combine this diet with regular exercise, stress management, and family time, then no doubt you will start cherishing enjoying each and every single day. If you suffer from any chronic conditions, then you can expect to see a great improvement over time. However, if you lack any one of these serious conditions, you can expect this diet and lifestyle to help you stay that way

www.ingramcontent.com/pod-product-compliance
Lightning Source LLC
Chambersburg PA
CBHW071354080526
44587CB00017B/3103